Wild Turkeys

Nature's Nervous Birds!

Love of Nature Series

ISSUE 23

Dr. Richard A. NeSmith

Applied Principles of Education & *Learning*

APE-Learning

© 2020 Richard A. NeSmith
Love of Nature Series

All Rights Reserved.

No part of this book may be reproduced, transmitted, or stored in any form or by any means except for your own personal use without the author's express, written permission. All graphs, drawings, and charts are created by the author or utilize public illustrations according to fair use for teaching, research, scholarship, and reporting. Some photos are those of the authors, and some are creative commons licensed. Special thanks to the following who contributed pro-bono from their collections.[i] Thank you all.

This book contains material used under the "Fair Use" of copyrighted material as provided for in section 107 of the U.S. Copyright Law. Every attempt has been made to provide credit to outside organizations or individuals who have provided images, illustrations, documents, or other information.

dr.nesmith@gmail.com

http://richardnesmith.obior.cc

All images in this book are copyright by their respective photographers.

Dr. Richard A. NeSmith
Winter Haven, FL 33884

DEC 2020

ISBN: 9798573962344

FLESCH-KINCAID GRADE LEVEL: 9.0

Wild Turkeys
(Meleagris *gallopavo*)

Turkeys are one of the most recognized game birds in North America. Most people have seen them, if not in the wild, at least on farms. Nearly every American schoolchild at some time has drawn or created art or crafts resembling wild turkeys. Such projects are especially true during the Thanksgiving season. These large birds were first domesticated as far back as the **Aztec Empire.**[1] For many

people, turkeys are menu specialties during national holidays.

INTRODUCTION TO AVES

Birds are fascinating warm-blooded, bi-pedal (two feet) animals noted under the Class **Aves.** Most birds can fly.

[1] 1428 A.D.

They have a backbone, feathers, lightweight hollow bones, and lungs with five or nine air sacs. The air sacs often extend into some of the bones. There are over 10,000 different bird species. Twenty percent of birds are known to migrate from one geographic region to another, though not so of the North American turkey.

There are *five major characteristics* of birds:

1. **feathers**
2. **wings**
3. **skeleton**
4. **beak**
5. **eggs**

These traits will help us understand turkeys as we learn about their range, habitat, reproduction, diet, and behavior.

The word "turkey" first appeared in the English language in the mid-1500s. Upon arriving in the New World, the English mistook the bird to be a "Turkish chicken." Therefore, when the Europeans came to North America, they saw a bird that looked like the guinea fowl. The word "turkey" since ancient times, meant "the land of the Turks." This American bird was misnamed, but the name remains to this day.

Turkeys are from the same biological family[2] in which are all heavy, ground-living birds (called **fowls**). Apart from turkeys, these include pheasants, partridges, quail, and chickens. Most of these are popular game birds or *game fowls* and have been favored by hunters for ages. There are five **subspecies**[3] of turkeys, but only one in North America,

---

[2] Phasianidae (pronounced: *phase ē on a di*)

[3] In scientific classification, the term *subspecies* refers to one of two or more populations of a species living in different subdivisions of the species. They vary from one another by morphological (outward traits) characteristics and often can breed and produce viable offspring.

and we simply called them *wild turkeys*.

Turkeys are large birds in the genus **Meleagris**[4], which are native to North America. The genus has two existing **species,** the Meleagris *gallopavo* and the Meleagris *ocellata*[5]. Only the *gallopavo* is found in North America.

From the *gallopavo* species come six **subspecies**[6]. These

---

[4] The term originated from Greek mythology where the goddess Artemis turned the grieving sisters of the slain **Meleager** into guinea fowls.

[5] The *ocellata* are wild turkeys of Central America's Yucatan Penisula.

[6] Term means they are very closely related and probably just isolated *geographically*.

very closely related birds include:

❶ **Eastern wild turkey**

❷ **Osceola wild turkey**

❸ **Rio Grande wild turkey**

❹ **Merriam's wild turkey**

❺ **Gould's wild turkey**

❻ **South Mexican wild turkey**

Range

Turkeys are presently thriving well in most parts of North America. Though their range is based on those isolated subspecies, they are found in every U.S. state except Alaska.

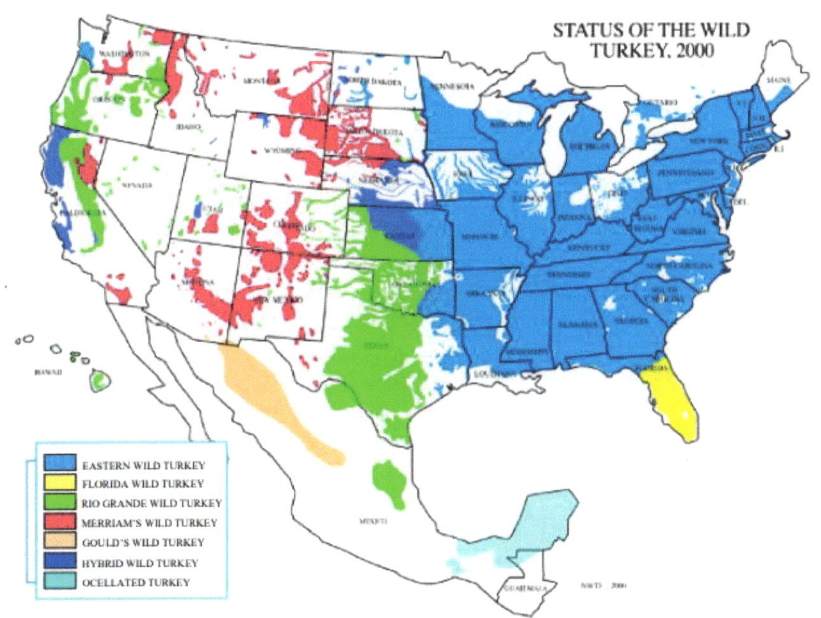

The **eastern wild turkey** is the original turkey subspecies

first viewed by the European settlers (Puritans, Jamestown settlers, and other early colonists). They have one of the largest ranges covering the entire eastern half of the United States (from Maine to north Florida and the Midwest, including Minnesota, Illinois, Missouri, and Canada). It is estimated that their population is just over 5 million birds.

The irony of the eastern wild turkey includes a story.
Western explorers often returned to England and Europe,

bringing back with them to the Old World the eastern wild turkeys. By 1620, when the Pilgrim settlers of Massachusetts brought imported European-raised [eastern] wild turkeys from England for food, they were totally unaware that the bird had a larger close relative already occupying the Massachusetts' forests.

The **Osceola wild turkeys**[7] are native to central and southern Florida, generally south of Orlando. In addition, there is an Osceola-Eastern turkey **hybrid** in Northern Florida. These birds number from 80,000 to 100,000.

The **Rio Grande wild turkey**, numbering approximately one million, are found from Texas to Oklahoma, Kansas, New Mexico, Utah, Colorado, Oregon and *introduced* to central and western California, a few northeastern states,

---

[7] This bird is named after the famous Seminole leader Osceola and was first described in 1890.

and Hawaii.

Merriam's wild turkeys range from the Rocky Mountains to the prairies of Wyoming, Montana, South Dakota, and the high plateaus of New Mexico, Arizona, Utah, and the Navajo Nation. These birds are estimated to be approaching 400,000.

The **Gould wild turkeys** are found from Mexico's central valleys and northern mountains, including the southernmost parts of Arizona and New Mexico. These tend to be the *largest in size* of the North American turkeys

but have the *smallest population* in total.

Finally, the **South Mexican wild turkey** (also called by its Spanish name, *guajolote*) is presented last, but it is not the least. It is believed to be the original stock from which the other five North American turkeys came.[8] It is one of the smallest turkeys. Their current population is unknown, and

---

[8] the ancestral lineage of our domesticate turkey

they are considered a ***critically* endangered species**.[9]

As we consider the range of North American wild turkeys, we need to stop a moment and learn valuable lessons from nature and **conservation**.[10] Wild turkeys have a much longer history on our continent than most animals. In the 1930s and '40s, these birds were on the brink of extinction. This decrease was partly due to overhunting, over-consumption, and poor conservation practices. We have since made necessary changes, including the founding of the

National Wild Turkey Federation in 1973. At that point, there were merely a total of 1.5 million turkeys in the wild. After nearly 50 years of wildlife management, the current turkey population is estimated to be approaching 6.2

---

[9] Also called the *ocellated turkey*, it was considered endangered by the Mexican endangered species list as recently as 2002 and has been assigned nearly threatened status by the IUCN in the year 2009. Despite a recent decline, they have begun to recover from the brink of extinction.
[10] Conservation is defined as "prevention of wasteful use of a resource."

million.

Characteristics

There is a story about how Benjamin Franklin wanted to make the United States national bird a turkey. Unfortunately, that story is not true and just another folktale. What Franklin actually did was write a letter complaining that the Bald Eagle was a poor choice for the honor.[11] He said the Great Seal image currently chosen *looked* like a turkey and that, in his view, he complimented the turkey as a *more respectable bird* than the eagle. Though he defended the turkey, he never proposed it as the National Bird.

A group of turkeys is called a **rafter** or a **flock**. The wild turkey is one of only two birds native to North America

---

[11] See the Franklin Institute article at: https://www.fi.edu/benjamin-franklin/franklin-national-bird#:~:text=The%20story%20about%20Benjamin%20Franklin,looked%20more%20like%20a%20turkey.

that has been regularly *domesticated*.[12] Domestic wild turkeys are now raised on farms and ranches worldwide for food and profit.

The male turkey is called a **tom** or a **gobbler** (due to the gobbling noise it frequently makes). The female is simply called a **hen**. Being so closely related, North American turkeys share many characteristics but have differences, including feather markings and body size.

Wild turkeys are large, ground-dwelling birds. They have powerful legs, fan-shaped tails, and a **wattle** hanging below their chin at the base of the neck. In addition, they have a tubular-like fleshy flap of skin that extends *over* the beak.[13] This is called a **snood**. It is a red fleshly lobe that can be extended or retracted to various sizes at will. The bare skin snood of the turkey's neck and its wattle are thought to

---

[12] The Muscovy Duck is the other.

[13] A snood can be short, sticking up like a horn, or long, extending past the nose. The size is controlled by the gobbler.

release excess heat on sweltering days.[14] However, its *primary* purpose may simply be to grab the attention of a mate. The snood turns bright red when the turkey is upset or during courtship. Both male and female wild turkeys have wattles, snoods, and spurs on their legs, but they are much more prominent and noticeable in the males (called **toms**).

The fleshy red, blue, yellow, or white bumps on the turkey's head and neck are called **carbuncles**. Male *gobblers* also have a ***beard*** made of black threadlike feathers coming from their breast. This "beard" almost looks out of place and is just a bunch or bundle of long skinny feathers and can grow so long as to touch the ground. Adult male turkeys and a small percentage of the females have beards. A turkey's beard resembles a horse's tail, except it's shorter and on the front of the body. Like the fleshy head carbuncle features, turkey beards are believed to be an

---

[14] If a turkey is ill, the wattle and snood will be very pale or almost white in color.

appealing feature intended to attract mates. Beards become more rigid when a tom is provoked. And, of course, there is the tom turkey's distinctive gobble sound, which can be heard a mile away.

There are approximately 5,500 feathers on an adult wild turkey, including 18 tail feathers that make up the male's distinct fan. Many of the feathers are iridescent, which gives the turkey its characteristic shimmering sheen. *Hens* tend to be smaller than males (called **sexual dimorphism**) and have ordinary, less extravagant feathers (**plumage**). Juvenile male turkeys are called **jakes** and have shorter tail feathers and shorter beards than the adult males. A full-grown gobbler turkey can measure up to four feet long and may weigh up to 30 pounds.[15]

Turkeys are one of the most alerted, alarmed, and anxious birds in the forest. They are **nature's nervous**

---

[15] Farmed or domestic turkeys are bred and fed for meat and profit so could weigh twice as much as a wild turkey.

birds and are always observing and ready to flee upon the first notice of anything unusual. They have great senses, including acute eyesight and keen hearing (despite not having external ear lobes). Wild turkeys see in color and have an excellent daytime vision. It is, in fact, three times

better than a human's eyesight and covers 270 degrees.[16] However, their sight at night is poor. Generally, they become even more cautious, suspicious, and nervous as nighttime approaches.

These turkeys have an uncanny ability to locate the source of a sound but must turn their head to see who or what they hear. A turkey's reflexes are remarkable. It can be standing still and jump into flight and be 40 yards away before a hunter can react to shoulder his gun. Wild turkeys have speedy reactions (some say it is ten times those of humans) and can run up to 20-30 miles per hour. Though

---

[16] A human's range is approximately 100° horizontally.

they can only fly 100 yards,[17] they can do so at 55 miles per hour. Wild turkeys are very agile and fly close to the ground but seldom for longer than a quarter of a mile.

More so than most animals, turkeys are routine creatures of habit. Though not precise, their travel routes are repetitive, and their flock will maintain the same general area. They become very familiar with their environment and what is *expected* and what is not. Their travel is led by food, water, and coverage when *scouting*.

A summary of the subspecies and their unique characteristics are noted in the table below.

	Range and Unique Features
❶ **Eastern wild turkey** (Meleagris *gallopavo silvestris*)	• chestnut-brown tips on tail feathers • white and black bars on the wings • adult males weigh 18 to 30 pounds; adult females weigh 8 to 12 pounds • very strong gobbles (strongest gobbles of all subspecies) • very long beards (longest beards of all subspecies) • important both to Native Americans and early Europeans in America. • important food source • provided feathers for head dressings and arrows. • Indians also used turkey spurs to make arrow points and other sharp utensils. • found in eastern North America • dark plumage with striking bronze, copper, and green iridescent colors
❷ **Osceola wild turkey** (Meleagris *gallopavo osceola*)	• often found in scrub patches of palmetto and occasionally near swamps, where amphibian prey is abundant.

---

[17] Breast muscles are white in color because they are filled with glycogen. This is the energy-carrying chemical that enriches the muscles so at to be able to flap the wings with great speed and stamina during flight. The short distance is directly linked to the glycogen being used up very quickly.

<table>
<tr><td>

</td><td>

- upper tail coverts are tipped with chestnut brown.
- males can reach 30 lbs. (14 kg) in weight
- is heavily hunted, and most hunted wild turkey subspecies
- smaller and darker than the eastern wild turkey
- wing feathers are very dark, with smaller amounts of the white barring seen on other subspecies. overall body feathers are an iridescent green-purple color
- weighing 16 to 18 pounds (7 to 8 kg)

</td></tr>
<tr><td>

❸ Rio Grande wild turkey

(Meleagris *gallopavo intermedia*)

</td><td>

- population estimates for this subspecies are around 1,000,000
- Subspecies id native to the central plain states
- first described in 1879
- has relatively long legs
- better adapted to a prairie habitat
- body feathers often have a green-coppery sheen
- tips of the tail and lower back feathers are a buff-to-very light tan color
- habitats include brush areas next to streams, rivers, mesquite, pine, and scrub oak forests
- very gregarious

</td></tr>
<tr><td>

❹ Merriam wild turkey

(Meleagris *gallopavo merriami*)

</td><td>

- found in the mountain forests of Colorado, New Mexico, and northern Arizona
- have been transplanted into the pine forests of Utah, Idaho, Washington, Oregon, California, Montana, Wyoming, Nebraska, and South Dakota and introduced into Oregon
- live in ponderosa pine mountainous regions
- named in 1900 in honor of Clinton Hart Merriam, the first chief of the U.S. Biological Survey
- tail and lower back feathers have white tips and purple and bronze reflections

</td></tr>
<tr><td>

❺ Gould wild turkey

(Meleagris *gallopavo Mexicana*)

</td><td>

- native to northwest Mexico and parts of southern Arizona and New Mexico
- the largest subspecies in body size of wild

</td></tr>
</table>

turkeys, but has the smallest population
• first described in 1856, in northern Mexico, and its range extended into the sky islands of southern Arizona and New Mexico
• heavily protected and regulated
• subspecies was first described in 1856
• exist in small numbers in the U.S. but are abundant in northwestern portions of Mexico.
• small population has been established in southern Arizona
• the largest of the six subspecies.
• have longer legs, larger feet, and longer tail feathers
• primary colors of the body feathers are copper and greenish-gold
• subspecies are heavily protected owing to their skittish nature and threatened status.

Habitat

Turkeys develop same-gender flocks of five to 50 individuals. Males run with males with some exceptions, including the breeding season. A rafter/flock will develop a 400 to 1,400 acre or more home range. This territory will be very diverse, including fields, pastures, farmland, meadows, woodlands, and swamps. Still, the territory will always contain a mixture of trees and grass cover. The range is determined by the amount of food these ecosystems provide.

Diet

Turkeys are ***opportunistic* omnivores**. Omnivores consume both plants and animals. In plants, they are particularly fond of nuts, including acorns, hickory nuts, beechnuts, and walnuts. They eat cracked or broken nuts or simply swallow them whole. Nuts are an especially welcomed means of survival during winter months when food sources are limited. They eat seeds, grain (including bird seed, corn, or wheat found in agricultural fields). They also seek different types of berries and fruits, including wild grapes, crabapples, etc. Fleshy plant parts are also sought after, such as buds, roots, bulbs, succulents, and cacti. Plant shrubbery, grass, and tender young leaves or shoots are also consumed.

A turkey's animal diet might include small reptiles, such as lizards and snakes, in addition to larger insects, including grasshoppers, spiders, and caterpillars. Snails, slugs, and earthworms provide additional nourishment.

Because turkeys do not have teeth, they will swallow their food whole. After food passes through the esophagus, it

moves into the **crop** (sometimes called a **craw**[18]). The crop is a thin-walled expanded portion of the alimentary tract used to store food before digestion. Food is stored in the crop before it moves into the **gizzard**. Turkeys pick up small particles of sand, stones, or gravel and swallow these for their gizzard to grind up their food not chewed. These dietary **organs** are found in a wide variety of animals,

---

[18] This organ has also been called ingluvies. It is a dilation or pouch in the esophagus of certain animals that receives food prior to the main stomach. See explanation provided in Love of Nature, Issue 17: *Barn Owls: Silent but Majestic.*

especially birds. A wild turkey can reach 25 lbs. in about four years.

Reproduction

Young hens mature and can produce offspring after 32 weeks. Toms seek out hens during the breeding season, which typically occurs in March and April. Both males and females tend to loosen their bonds with their respective flocks during mating season.

Gobblers will mate with as many hens as they can, and this predominant male is established through intimidation, scuffles, and even "turkey fights." Males seek to attract females with their array of colorful carbuncles, snood, wattle, and, finally, *strutting*. This behavior is almost a *dance-like ritual* where they fan out their tail feathers, drag their wings on the ground, throwback their head, and quickly and rapidly step.

The females become more solitary and secretive in May when it comes to nesting. The hen will begin to wander off from the flock and become more isolated as she finds a remote place for her nest, as well as during those times when she begins to lay her clutch.[19] Mated hens will begin scratching out nests on the ground in small depressions in places of their liking. These nests are only protected by the surrounding dense camouflage of the brush, grass, and the hen's perfect blended-colored plumage. She will lay an egg and then return to the flock repeatedly until the last egg is laid when she then begins incubation.[20] Females will lay only one egg *per day* for up to two weeks. This strategy produces from four to 14 eggs, which she will

incubate for four to five weeks. Males have no paternal responsibilities for the offspring and provide no care or support.

Hens keep a close eye on their nest. These newly hatched turkeys are called **poults**. If something gets too close, they will make an alarm call and try to lead the predator away by making a big *fleeing* display. This act is done to divert the intruder's attention away from the location of the nest.

---

[19] A clutch of eggs is the group of eggs produced by birds, amphibians, or reptiles, often at a single time, particularly those laid in a nest.

[20] The turkey egg will remain dormant until incubation begins.

Ten to 40 to 50 percent of eggs successfully hatch. But, only about 25 percent of hatching poults will make it beyond four weeks. Turkeys do have predators, and foxes, coyotes, cougars, eagles, and hawks are always a threat.

However, the most danger lies in the predation of their eggs. Snakes, skunks, crows and ravens, opossums, raccoons, and dogs are all delighted to feast on turkey eggs.

Poults usually hatch in June. Recently hatched turkeys are not called chicks because *chicks* are "born" **altricial** (featherless, blind, cold, helpless, and needing to be

continually fed). This feature is not so with turkey hatchlings. Being born on the ground in the wild requires offspring to be ready to go, run, and feed almost instantly. Otherwise, they would be easy prey for predators. Instead, turkey hatchlings are **precocial**,[21] as are ducks,[22] geese, and grouse.

One might say that precocial birds grow up fast. Within

---

[21] A precocial bird is capable of moving around on its own soon after hatching, meaning it has its feathers in place, and instinctively can feed itself. The word comes from the same Latin root as *precocious*.

[22] See Love of Nature, Issue 20: *Mallards & Wood Ducks: Grace and Beauty on Water*.

one hour of hatching, they are alert and active. Young wild
turkeys, from two to four days old, dust, sun, and preen

just like the adults. However, during the first three to four weeks of life, baby turkeys cannot fly and rely on their mother for protection.

Like most birds that produce *precocial offspring,* there is a phenomenon called **synchronous hatching**. The key to synchronizing the hatching for turkeys focuses on *when* incubation begins. This synchronizing feature does not initiate until incubation, which does not usually begin *until all the eggs are laid.* In other words, the embryos in these eggs will not begin to develop until the hen starts incubating them. Four weeks later, the eggs hatch. That is a dangerous time for the hen as she is nearly defenseless.

As a result of synchronous hatching, the clutch's eggs are born within an hour or two of each other even though they have been laid days apart. All the poults hatching within an hour of one another ensures a higher survival rate and less chance of nest predation.

Precocial birds are hatched with their *eyes open* and covered in *down feathers.* They can quickly leave the nest within 12 to

24 hours, and in fact, they must be able to do so to feed. The poults will follow their mom around while she is pointing out food during foraging. Immediate activity for poults is useful because turkey flocks often cover many miles in a day while foraging. The poults have to keep up with the mother hen as she leads them through her flock's territory, searching for food and avoiding predators.

Poults benefit from the hen's intuitive nature of protecting them. From four to five weeks old, poults begin to fly 25 to 50 feet. At this time, they can join the hen for roosting in trees, depending on the sub-species, location, and temperature. Most survival tactics are learned by imitating older birds (**mimicry**). They eventually learn how to find food and navigate the boundaries of their home range on their own.

Turkeys may use traditional roost sites night after night, but they generally use different sites and move from tree to tree. Even after poults take to **roosting** in the trees at night, these young turkeys will stay with their mother for another four or five months, or until the next mating season. As the poults mature, they become known as **jakes** (males) and **jennies** (females). When gobblers sit on the roost, they tend to be more vocal because they feel safe from

predators, and often they are calling and trying to locate the rest of their flock.

The lifespan of a wild turkey is three to five years but less than ten. Their domesticated cousins can live much longer. The longest recorded lifespan for a turkey in captivity is 12 years four months.

Behavior

Turkeys are **diurnal**, meaning they are most active and about during daylight hours. On any given day, they are most lively during calm, clear days in the early morning and early afternoon hours. A turkey's activity generally decreases with bad weather conditions, including wind and rain. During storms, very wet and rainy days, turkeys are neither vocal nor very active.

We know that turkeys are creatures of routine. They do have a daily predictable manner which they carry through, including eating, breeding, dusting, and loafing. It may be

that the routine heightens their awareness of any changes in their habitat. Successful turkey hunters tend to learn these habits.

Dusting tends to be a flock activity. As these birds preen (repair and perform feather maintenance), they will seek dust baths. Locating a dirt-sandy location, they will lower themselves crouched to the ground and flap frantically, spreading dust over their bodies. This ritual may help in reducing mites and other parasites. The primary purpose, however, is to prevent the feathers from becoming greasy or matted.

Often **sunning** and preening follow a dust bath as part of the grooming procedure. Sunning turkeys rest on one side and spread the upward wing and leg to expose a large surface area to direct sunlight. Turkeys (and other birds) tend to sun for any of four possible reasons:

1. adding body warmth during cold days
2. maintaining healthy feathers
3. removing parasites and possibly harmful bacteria and fungi
4. relaxation

Preening is a typical bird behavior. The bird will remove dust, dirt, and parasites and are meticulously reattaching and reconnect the microscopic interlocking hooks, called **barbs**, at the edge of each feather strand. Under normal wear, these come disconnected and can inhibit flight. Preening also involves moving oil from the preening gland (**uropygial gland**) and spreading it over the feathers. This oil provides a waterproof coating and keeps feathers soft and flexible. It has now also been found to have disinfectant[23] properties, reducing illness or chances of disease. Preening is a regular routine and ritual and ensures

a quick getaway during flight.

Turkeys **molt** twice a year. Molting is the biological process in which a bird sheds feathers to replace and grow new ones. Molting is regulated by hormones and is quite common. Birds are susceptible to danger and predation during the molting period, for it requires a great deal of energy to grow new feathers. Until they do, they are unable to fly. The complete annual molt occurs during the summer

---

[23] antimicrobial

and early autumn, following the breeding season.

While turkeys spend most of their time on the ground during the day, they sleep in trees at night. This practice is a crucial component of a wild turkey's survival. They will often select the largest trees and roost as high as they can comfortably perch at dusk. Hardwood trees (oaks, maples, hickories, beech, and birch) seem to be preferred. Sleeping in trees means protection from predators that roam at night. At dusk, they fly back down to the ground to begin their daily routine. As a general rule of thumb, turkeys are most active during calm, clear days in the morning and early afternoon hours. Rainy days, wind, and storms encourage them to stay in their roosts longer than usual.

Just as chickens and other ground birds have a *pecking order*, so do turkeys. A hierarchy is formed with clear dominant individuals for both males and females. Usually, the older birds lead, but there are exceptions such as poor health or fitness. Turkeys are very **territorial** and will fight one another.

Wild turkeys in North America do not migrate. Instead, they establish geographical areas and, with some crossbreeding, remain. In the cold and snowy north, these birds must learn how to select the best and largest conifer trees where they can fly onto the branches for shelter during blizzards. Once

the weather calms, they will continue foraging.

Turkeys do communicate, or *talk turkey*! They have 28 distinct calls, and each sound has a meaning used for different situations. Of course, toms are notorious for the gobble sounds, which have a fixed intensity, unlike the other sounds.

The adult hen has an assembly call made up of loud yelps, usually a little more emphatic and longer than a standard series of yelps. A hen uses this assembly yelp to assemble her flock or young poults. It is a useful call in the fall when trying to call a scattered flock back together.

Turkey calls have been copied and simulated with various tools and mouthpieces by hunters and turkey enthusiasts for some time. Turkey calls have been cataloged, and a few of them include the following:

Turkey Sounds	
❶ **clucks**	One or more short staccato notes; generally used by one bird to get the attention of another and can bring a gobbler to an awaiting hen.
❷ **cluck & purr**	Followed by a rolling staccato call. Associated with *flock talk* or feeling of contentment and reassures the flock. Not loud, but can be amplified.
❸ **cutt**	Loud and sharp clucks; often mixed with yelping. Indicates excitement but not alarm. Sometimes used by hunters to mimic callbacks to another encroaching hen back for a contest.
❹ **excited yelp**	Similar to a plain yelp but more intense, excited, and louder. Indicates that a turkey is upset over something.
❺ **fly-down or fly-up cackle**	Three to ten irregularly spaced notes, loud and staccato, higher-pitched as a call nears its end. Often indicates leaving the roost or time to head up to the roost.

❻ gobble	Loud, rapid gurgling sound made by a tom; principal vocalization of the male, used primarily in the spring to let the hens know he is in the area.

Miscellaneous

Tom turkeys, running in their own flock most of the year. They are seldom seen except during the mating season. This may be due to their flocks being smaller in number or their ability to hide in the bushes where their natural coloring makes them just about invisible. Regardless, more female flocks are generally the ones reported by observers. More often than not, the toms are only seen during mating season or when they tend to "fatten up" in autumn before the winter months in more open pine and beechnut forests, munching on acorns.

Wild turkeys are thriving in most locations now, but that

was not always the case. By the 1930s Great Depression, and following World War II, North American turkeys were on the brink of extinction, with just 30,000 wild turkeys remaining. This was partly due to ❶ a lack of laws protecting wild game, and ❷ lack of designated hunting seasons, so many families hunted them for their own survival needs. Along with poor management issues, such as unspecified burns during egg-laying season, all played a toll on turkeys. Finally, conser-vationists created programs[24] to help monitor and restore the population of

wild turkeys. After 40 years of effort, their number has reached a historic high of about 6.7 million turkeys. However, today that number is down. According to biology researchers, there may be four possible explanations for the current decline:

1. **Production, not predation, drives turkey populations.**

2. **With high population densities, a significant number of hens won't access quality nesting habitat and may not successfully hatch or raise a brood.**

3. **Carrying capacity becomes an issue, and productivity is declining because hens are nesting in suboptimal habitats.**

4. **Vegetation measurements contribute to nesting sites' success or failure; little vegetation means little chance at poult survival.**

Carrying capacity is defined *as the number or quantity of*

---

[24] The passing of the 1937 Wildlife Restoration Act saved the turkey population.

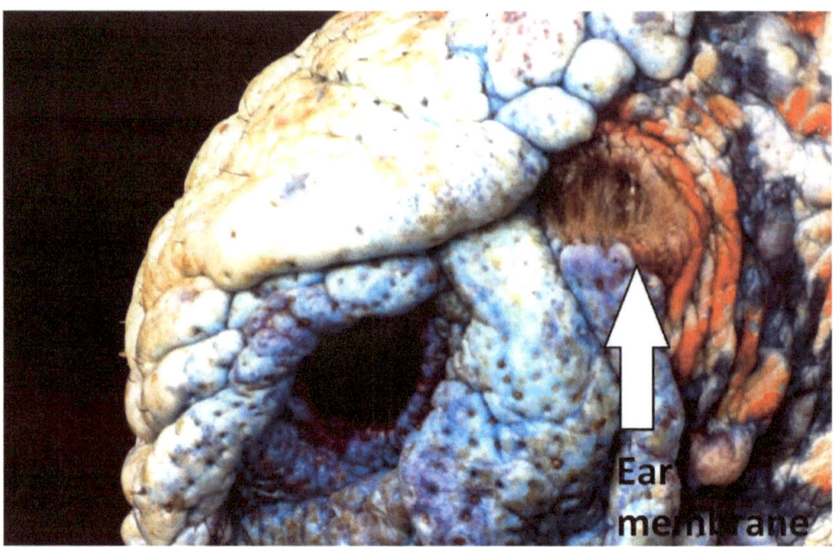

animals that can successfully be conveyed or held in an environment without destroying the environment or decreasing the population. In some geographical regions, the turkeys are reaching carrying capacity but have declined as the capacity of the habitat decline. If the habitat conditions decline across multiple counties and states, turkeys have no choice but to decline in number.

Estimates suggest the turkey population today is between 6–6.2 million birds. The fact that the overall turkey count dropped almost 15 percent may indicate that these birds still warrant close monitoring.

When the first unofficial presidential pardons were granted to domestic turkeys is in dispute. Some suggest it literally started when in 1863, President Abraham Lincoln's turkey was brought to the White House, but Tad, Lincoln's son, interceded on its behalf, and so its life was spared. Others argue that the tradition began in 1947 by Franklin D. Roosevelt. And some now even claim it was George H.W. Bush who started the tradition. Whoever did it, every president since has "pardoned" two birds (a presidential turkey and a vice-presidential turkey) before Thanksgiving. The pardoned birds live out their days on different farms. They are often put on display temporarily for the American public to greet.

Also, national attention again spotlights turkeys as June is National Turkey Lovers' Month and promotes eating turkey at times other than major holidays. Turkey meat is low in fat and high in protein, making it healthier than many types of meat. The average American eats 18 pounds of turkey every year. More turkeys are consumed on Thanksgiving than on Christmas and Easter combined.[25]

We have come to know and appreciate wild turkeys because they are delicious to eat. They represent a healthy part of our history. And they are only occasionally seen in the wild. It may be that being the most hunted bird in North America, they have an excellent reason for being **nature's nervous bird**.

---

[25] Most turkeys consumed in the United States are not wild turkeys, but rather domesticated, farm-grown turkeys.

REVIEW

1. Who was the first to domesticate the turkey?

2. Explain what turkey is the original North American turkey and its current status.

3. List the five characteristics of the class Aves?

4. Why did the American colonists call this large ground bird a *turkey*?

5. From the map on page 7, which turkey has the most extensive range?

6. Which subspecies of turkey is the largest in body size?

7. What are wattle and a snood, and what purpose do we think they serve?

8. How far can a turkey fly?

9. What is a gizzard, and what purpose does it have?

10. If a juvenile male turkey is called a jake then what is a juvenile female turkey called?

WILD TURKEY HEN

COLORING PAGE

http://www.supercoloring.com/coloring-pages/wild-turkey-hen

Name:_______________________

Wild Turkeys: Nature's Nervous Birds

Carefully read each statement and place the answer in the correct boxes. Use the Word Bank if needed.

Created using the Crossword Maker on TheTeachersCorner.net

poults   roosting   molting   precocial,   federation   gobbler   domesticated   Mexico

Gould   gizzard   jennie   barbs   Osceola   rafter

Across

3. Big male turkey
9. When a bird has been 'tamed.'
11. With tiny rocks to help break up food.
13. Losing feathers at a particular time of the year.
14. Group of turkeys

Down

1. The small total population turkey in North America?
2. microscopic interlocking hooks
4. It's a Florida turkey.
5. Name for a young hen
6. Sleeping in trees.
7. Poults are born with feathers, alert, and ready to travel within hours.
8. National Wild Turky ___________.
10. The original North American turkey from which all the others came is probably the Sout ______ wild turkey.
12. Hatching turkeys?

44

INTERESTING SOURCES TO CONSIDER

Finding a wild turkey nest. Available at:
https://youtu.be/ebRspiQED7Y

Guide to North American Birds. Audubon. Available at:
https://www.audubon.org/field-guide/bird/wild-turkey

History of the Wild Turkey in North America. Available at:
https://www.mdwfp.com/media/4016/historywildturkeynortham
erica.pdf

Meet Your North American Wild Turkeys. Available at:
https://bowhunting360.com/2020/03/12/meet-your-north-
american-wild-turkeys/

Return of the Wild Turkey (1970). Available at:
https://youtu.be/TOJQnlDidzs

Subspecies of North American Wild Turkey. Outdoor Alabama.
Available at: https://www.outdooralabama.com/wild-
turkey/subspecies-north-american-wild-turkey

The American Turkey. Kidzone Animal Facts. Available at:
https://www.kidzone.ws/ANIMALS/turkey.htm

Turkey (Birds) Facts for Kids. Kiddle. Available at:
https://kids.kiddle.co/Turkey_(bird)

Wild Turkey Basics. National Wild Turkey Federation. Available at:
https://www.nwtf.org/hunt/wild-turkey-basics

Wild Turkey Documentary: America s National Bird Films. Available at:
https://youtu.be/udyRkz0tWZc

Wild Turkey Documentary: America s National Bird Films. Available at:
https://youtu.be/udyRkz0tWZc

Wild Turkey Fight. Available at: https://youtu.be/l-f8PbLbIXc

Wild Turkey Sounds. Available at: https://www.nwtf.org/hunt/wild-
turkey-basics/turkey-sounds

Wild Turkeys Dusting in Summer. Available at:
https://youtu.be/qYnnSHsEcjA

Wild Turkeys Roosting with Babies (Poults). Available at:
https://youtu.be/7nCYXdr4M7Y

Wild Turkeys: What Do They Look Like? BioKids. Available at:
http://www.biokids.umich.edu/critters/Meleagris_gallopavo/

ABOUT THE AUTHOR

Richard NeSmith is a native of Florida, USA. He grew up wading through the swamps of central Florida with his two younger brothers during the pre-Disney era, and unknowingly, falling in love with biology, wildlife, and nature. He has lived in seven American states, twice in Australia, and once in Mexico City. He holds eight university degrees and has taught for 14 years in secondary schools, here and abroad, and another 13 years as a professor in several American universities. His service includes professor of science education, Dean of Education, Campus Dean, as well as an online instructor. His passion for learning (and *how we learn*) did not develop until *after* graduating from high school. His only explanation for this is that *having a goal made all the difference in the world*. He enjoys reading, hiking, nature photography, golf, and tennis.

http://richardnesmith.obior.cc

Applied **P**rinciples of **E**ducation & Learning *presents*

***APE*-Learning**

AMAZON AUTHOR's PAGE:

https://www.amazon.com/author/richardnesmith

Educational, wildlife, and naturalist books
Dr. Richard NeSmith.

Issue 1
Raccoons:
Friendly Bandits
Dr. Richard NeSmith

Issue 2
Sandhill Cranes
&
Pileated Woodpeckers
Flaming Redheads
Dr. Richard NeSmith

Issue 3
American
Alligators
&
Crocodiles
Dr. Richard NeSmith

Issue 4
Bobcats:
Ghostly Elusive
Dr. Richard NeSmith

Issue 5
Foxes:
Sneaky Rascals
Dr. Richard NeSmith

Issue 6
Armadillo:
Little Armored One
Dr. Richard NeSmith

Issue 7
Squirrels:
Bushy Tail Scampers
Dr. Richard NeSmith

Issue 8
River Otters:
Aquatic Clowns !
Dr. Richard NeSmith

Issue 9
Beavers:
Nature's Engineers !
Dr. Richard NeSmith

Issue 10
Black Bears
Titans of the Forest
Dr. Richard NeSmith

Issue 11
Freshwater
Turtles
Dr. Richard NeSmith

Issue 12
FUNGI, LICHENS
& MUSHROOMS
Dr. Richard NeSmith

Paperbacks: http://amazon.com/author/richardnesmith

e-books: https://bit.ly/3iuCgB3

---

[i] **Special thanks to the following who kindly provided permission to use their photographs.**

From Unsplash: Kirk Thornton, Marcel Langthim, Diane Olivier, Chalaphan Mathong, Dulcey Lima, Ruth Caron, and Hermes Rivera.

From Pixaby: Steve Raubenstine, Daina Krumins, Nadine Doerlé, Manfred Antranias Zimmer, Jim Bradley, and the prolific skeeze.

Also, special thanks to **Cindy Frasier**, **Kerry Bower**, **Lou Albrecht**, **Heather Wolken**, **Bev Carr**, **Greg Jowers**, **Tom Dotson**, and **Stacey Diamond** for their graciously sharing of some photographs of these beautiful creatures.

Thank you, everyone.

Love Learning —Love Nature—Love Living

www.ingramcontent.com/pod-product-compliance
Lightning Source LLC
Chambersburg PA
CBHW040238240726
48664CB00001B/176